D0934358

WORLD'S SCARIEST PLACES

SPOOKY HOTELS

ALIX WOOD

 Gareth Stevens
PUBLISHING

Please visit our website, **www.garethstevens.com**. For a free color catalog of all
our high-quality books, call toll free 1-800-542-2595 or fax 1-877-542-2596

Cataloging-in-Publication Data
Names: Wood, Alix.
Title: Spooky hotels / Alix Wood.
Description: New York : Gareth Stevens, 2017. | Series: World's scariest places | Includes index.
Identifiers: ISBN 9781482459166 (pbk.) | ISBN 9781482459180 (library bound) |
  ISBN 9781482459173 (6 pack)
Subjects: LCSH: Haunted hotels--Juvenile literature. | Haunted places--Juvenile literature. | Ghosts--
  Juvenile literature.
Classification: LCC BF1474.5 W66 2017 | DDC 133.1'22--dc23

First Edition

Published in 2017 by
Gareth Stevens Publishing
111 East 14th Street, Suite 349
New York, NY 10003

Copyright © 2017 Gareth Stevens Publishing

Produced for Gareth Stevens by Alix Wood Books
Designed by Alix Wood
Editor: Eloise Macgregor

Photo credits: Cover, 1, 3, 4, 13, 25 © AdobeStock; 5 top © James Stringer; 5 bottom © Thomas
Quine; 6-7 © Kiral; 7 top © Dianna A; 7 bottom, 14-15, 23 bottom © Shutterstock; 8-9 © Henry
Stewart; 10-11 © Jason Mrachina; 11 top © Warrior Squirrel; 12 © Robert Nyman; 15 top © Hank
Jeffers; 16 © Anders P. Ahlström; 17 top © Udo Schröter; 17 bottom © Cami 1973; 18 © NSW State
Records; 19 © Henrietta Phillips; 20-21, 23 top, 27 © public domain; 21 top © DollarPhotoClub; 22
© HistoryStuff2; 24-25 © Luke Ma; 26 © Langham Hotels International; 28 © S. Gerbic; 29 top ©
Patricia Henry

All rights reserved. No part of this book may be reproduced in any form without permission from
the publisher, except by reviewer.

Printed in China

CPSIA compliance information: Batch #CW17GS. For further information contact
Gareth Stevens, New York, New York at 1-800-542-2595.

Contents

When a hotel is hundreds of years old, just think how many people may have slept in the same room as you! People may have died there, or murdered someone in that very room. Sometimes, the hotel is built on an already haunted site. The hotel can also have previously been a castle or grand old house. With all that history, it's not surprising hotels are sometimes said to be haunted.

A ghost is thought to be the spirit of a dead person. Not everyone believes ghosts are real. Many people who don't believe in ghosts still think some buildings are plain creepy, though. Step inside these hotels and see what YOU think.

Guests can spend the night at the scarily-named Chillingham Castle, if they dare. Rumor has it this beautiful, ancient English castle is home to several ghosts. In the Pink Room, terrified guests have been woken by flashes of blue lights. The castle also has its own **torture** chamber! The chair on the right doesn't look too comfortable.

Banff Springs Hotel, Canada

The majestic Banff Springs Hotel in Alberta, Canada, is said to be home to several ghosts. Some are helpful, such as the ghost of a former **bellman** who likes to help guests to their rooms. He has been known to turn lights on and off and even unlock doors. However, if you speak to him, or offer him a tip, he vanishes! Other ghosts are not so friendly. Room 873 had to be sealed shut after so many reports of strange events happening in there.

A man murdered his wife and young daughter in room 873, and then killed himself. Since that day, people say they have heard shrieks in the night. Chambermaids also reported finding bloody fingerprints on the mirror that would not wash off!

Local legend says that in the 1930s a bride and groom were holding their wedding party at the hotel. As the bride walked up the stairs to the ballroom, her dress brushed a candle, and caught fire. In her panic she tripped, fell down the stairs, and broke her neck.

Since that day, her ghost is said to haunt the hotel. People have sighted her dancing in the ballroom, or walking up the staircase.

The Ancient Ram Inn, England

Believed to be the most haunted hotel in Britain, the Ancient Ram Inn in Gloucestershire is a terrifying place to stay. The present owner describes being pulled out of bed and dragged across the room on his first night at the property! Guests have often left in the middle of night, scared out of their wits. They experienced mysterious voices, ghostly figures, and being touched or pulled. Visitors have also felt a strong sense of evil at the Inn.

While working on repairing the floor, the owners disturbed an ancient grave. The inn was believed to have been built on a **pagan** burial area. Two children's skeletons were found, alongside two ancient daggers. Some believe the children were killed in a kind of pagan ritual. Guests have said they have heard the sound of children screaming while staying at the inn.

The attic is said to be haunted by a local wanted criminal, William Crewe, who used to hide there when he visited the village. He was later hung for his crimes. The attic is also said to be the site where an innkeeper's daughter was murdered. The ghost of a young girl, a **monk**, and a witch have also reportedly been seen at the inn.

Many local people will cross the street at night rather than walk past the creepy inn!

The Queen Mary Hotel, Long Beach

O nce a British ocean liner, the RMS Queen Mary is now a luxury hotel. It is **moored** at Long Beach, California. It is thought to be one of America's most haunted hotels! Cabin B340 is no longer rented out, as guests have experienced faucets turning on by themselves, and bedsheets flying across the room!

Captain Jones, the last captain to sail the *Queen Mary*, loved a good cigar. Passenger Winston Churchill also loved cigars. Guests often report the sudden, unexplained smell of cigar smoke near the stairs and the staterooms.

ONE OF THE SHIP'S POOLS

The ship's two swimming pools are both believed to be haunted. A woman in a 1930s bathing suit is often seen walking around the pool and then vanishing. Wet footprints have been seen on the poolside.

Guests report that a young girl can sometimes be heard laughing and playing in one of the pools. Some people believe she may have drowned there although there is no evidence in the **ship's log** of anyone having drowned on the ship.

Airth Castle, Scotland

This ancient 14th century Scottish castle is now a fine hotel. It is a peaceful place to stay, unless you get room 3, 9, or 23! These rooms are all said to be haunted by the sound of children playing.

Visitors say they have seen doors open and close by themselves. Some people have reported seeing objects moving around on their own. A man's dusty footprints have appeared on a blocked-off staircase. The footprints are believed to belong to a long-dead **groundsman** who worked at the castle! He is sometimes seen haunting the lower floor.

AIRTH CASTLE

The ghost of the castle's old **housekeeper** has been reported by several people. The housekeeper is believed to have been looking after two young children. Her carelessness is thought to have led to the two children dying in a fire.

Her spirit has been seen with the ghosts of the two young children, too. They are said to be a girl around 6 years of age and a boy of about 9 years. They may be the children heard playing in the bedrooms.

A phantom dog has been felt at Airth Castle. The dog brushes past people's legs, and occasionally it gives them a little nip on the ankle!

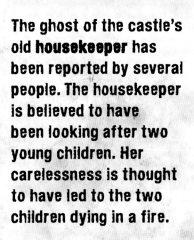

Hotel Burchianti, Italy

The Burchianti is a fashionable small hotel in the beautiful city of Florence, Italy. Poets, artists, and the former Italian leader, Benito Mussolini, have all stayed at the hotel. It has also become famous for being one of Florence's most haunted hotels.

Guests say they have seen ghostly children skipping down the corridors. Sitting in one of the hotel's armchairs in the entrance hall, a phantom old lady has been seen busily knitting! A ghostly maid has also been seen at night, moving from room to room, cleaning.

Italian dictator, Mussolini, is said to have once stayed in the beautifully decorated fresco room. Guests staying there have reported feeling as if they were being watched. Some have said they also felt cold breath on their faces!

THE FLORENCE SKYLINE AT SUNSET

Toftaholm Herrgård, Sweden

An old manor house once lay on the site of this beautiful Swedish hotel. The ruins can still be seen today. Built in the 1400s, it was the home to a wealthy family. They bought the village and forced the local farmers out of their farms in order to build the first manor house! That may have led to some unhappy local spirits.

The hotel has an exciting history. Gustav Vasa, later King Gustav I of Sweden, once hid from the Danes at Toftaholm manor.

THE MAIN HOTEL WAS BUILT IN 1871

RUINS OF THE OLD MANOR

The hotel is believed to be haunted by a young local peasant. He was in love with the daughter of the house. She was made to marry someone her family had chosen, instead. On the morning of the wedding, the heartbroken man hanged himself from the rafters. Visitors to the hotel have heard strange noises. Doors and windows also sometimes shut by themselves.

The Russell Hotel, Australia

If you check in to room 8 at the Russell Hotel you may find you are not alone. During the night, the ghost of a sailor has been seen standing at the foot of the bed staring at the guests! The hotel is one of the oldest buildings in Australia. The area of Sydney where the hotel stands was once home to visiting sailors who moored at the docks. It is believed the sailor that haunts room 8 may have been murdered there.

Senior police officer Henry Murrow was murdered right outside the hotel in 1897. Daniel Conway (right) was drunk and cursing in the street. When Murrow intervened he was struck and hit his head on the pavement. He later died. Conway went to jail. Could Murrow or Conway be causing the mysterious footsteps often heard in the hotel's hallways?

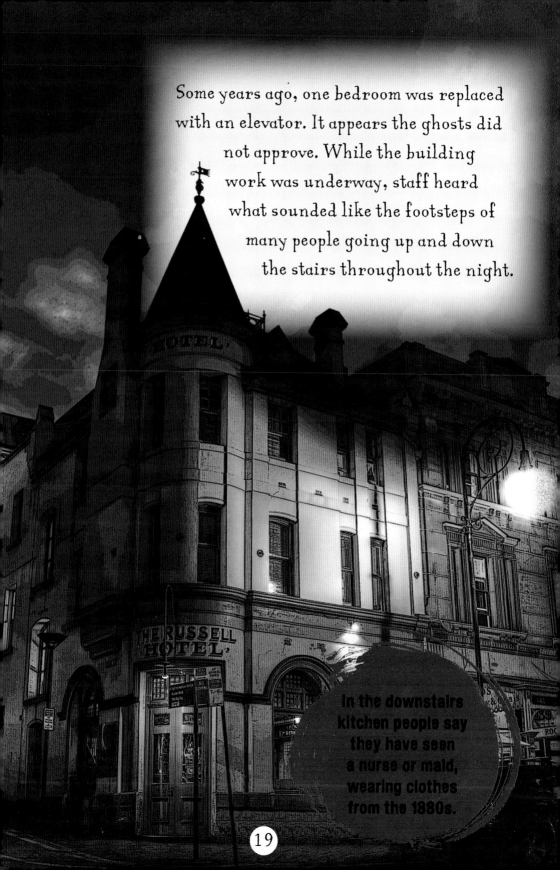

Some years ago, one bedroom was replaced with an elevator. It appears the ghosts did not approve. While the building work was underway, staff heard what sounded like the footsteps of many people going up and down the stairs throughout the night.

In the downstairs kitchen people say they have seen a nurse or maid, wearing clothes from the 1880s.

19

Shelbourne Hotel, Ireland

The Shelbourne Hotel, Dublin, was built in 1824 on the site of a row of houses. A little girl has been said to haunt one of the rooms in the hotel. In 1965, famous ghost hunter, Hans Holzer, and his wife, Sybil Leek, believed they made contact with the ghost. She told Leek that her name was Mary Masters and she was looking for her sister, Sophie.

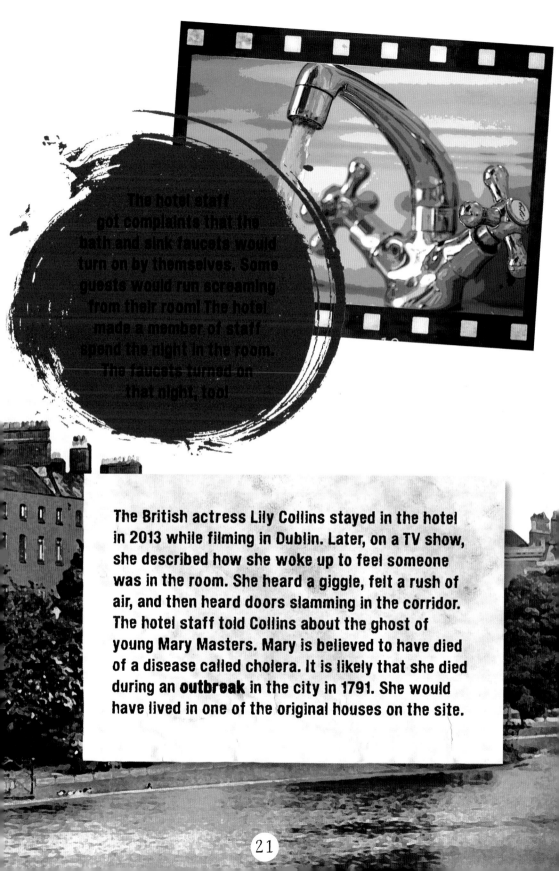

The hotel staff
got complaints that the
bath and sink faucets would
turn on by themselves. Some
guests would run screaming
from their room! The hotel
made a member of staff
spend the night in the room.
The faucets turned on
that night, too!

The British actress Lily Collins stayed in the hotel in 2013 while filming in Dublin. Later, on a TV show, she described how she woke up to feel someone was in the room. She heard a giggle, felt a rush of air, and then heard doors slamming in the corridor. The hotel staff told Collins about the ghost of young Mary Masters. Mary is believed to have died of a disease called cholera. It is likely that she died during an **outbreak** in the city in 1791. She would have lived in one of the original houses on the site.

Hotel Chelsea, New York

The Chelsea is one of the best-known hotels in New York. It is also one of the most haunted! Many well-known people have stayed there, and some have also died there!

Punk rock musician Sid Vicious stayed there with his girlfriend, Nancy. She was found stabbed to death in the bathroom of room 100, and Sid was arrested for murder.

Sid Vicious killed himself while waiting to be tried for Nancy's murder. Both he and Nancy are now said to haunt the hotel.

Hotel Chelsea

A lady named Mary survived the tragic sinking of the RMS *Titanic* in 1912, and came to live at the Chelsea. Sadly, her husband had died in the disaster. Not wanting to live without him, she hanged herself in her room. Her ghost is said to still wander around the hotel, looking at herself in any mirrors close to her old apartment.

Room 206 is supposed to be one of the most haunted rooms in the hotel. Welsh poet and writer Dylan Thomas died in the room, in 1953. People say his ghost has frequently been seen in the room and the corridor. Others have heard loud footsteps outside the door of room 206.

Akasaka Weekly Mansion, Japan

The busy, modern city of Tokyo, Japan, is not somewhere you would expect to come across a haunted hotel. However, Building 1 at the Akasaka Weekly Mansion has had many guests running to check out early.

Visitors have woken up feeling as if someone is touching them or stroking their hair! Others complain of ghostly figures standing at the foot of their beds. Strange mist has been seen slipping out of the rooms' air vents. People also complain that the room suddenly feels cold.

One of the scariest stories from the mansion was from a woman who woke up to find she was being dragged across the room by her hair. She was even said to have scratches on her back the following morning!

The Akasaka Weekly Mansion was completely remodeled in 2016 and is now called Hotel Mystays Akasaka. Perhaps the new name and decor will keep the ghosts away!

A few guests are said to have experienced a very unusual sight. They have woken up to see a ghostly woman crawling around the bedroom!

THE TOKYO SKYLINE

The Langham Hotel, England

London's Langham Hotel was built in 1865. It is said to be the home to several ghosts. Room 333 appears to be the most haunted room. A guest in that room may have been pushed out of bed in the night by an unknown force! Visitors think a **butler** has been seen wandering the corridors in his undarned socks. The ghost of a German prince who committed suicide by jumping from a window has been seen barging through doors in the early hours, too.

THE LANGHAM, LONDON

Another ghost said to haunt the hotel is that of a man with a gaping hole in his face! He often has been seen in the hallways.

England **cricketer**, Stuart Broad, experienced a creepy event when the team was staying at the Langham. During the night the faucets suddenly came on in the bathroom. When he turned the light on, the faucets turned themselves off. When he turned the light off again, the faucets came back on. He quickly switched rooms!

A doctor is said to have killed his new wife while on his honeymoon at the hotel. The doctor then killed himself. His ghost has been seen in room 333. Guests who have seen him say that at first he appears as a glowing ball and then turns into the shape of a man. His legs are incomplete and he floats around the room with a blank stare.

The Stanley Hotel, Colorado

The Stanley Hotel was first run by a Mr. and Mrs. Stanley. Though they have both died, it appears that they have not yet left the building! The ghost of Mr. Stanley has been seen standing behind staff at the **reception** desk.

An old housekeeper, Elizabeth Wilson, is said to also still haunt the hotel. She was hurt in an explosion at the hotel but continued to work there until her old age. Apparently she still turns up for work. Guests have found their bags unpacked, and their sheets turned down by an invisible presence!

THE HAUNTED PIANO

Some say Mrs. Stanley has been heard playing her much-loved piano in the hotel's music room at night.

The Stanley Hotel's spooky atmosphere inspired well-known horror writer Stephen King to write a best-selling book about a deserted hotel. He and his wife stayed there one night, just as the hotel was about to close for the season.

The couple discovered that they were the only guests in the vast hotel. King found the long corridors and empty dining room very creepy. He planned the whole plot for his book that day. The hotel certainly made a perfect setting for a horror story.

Glossary

bellman A hotel employee who takes guests to rooms, carries luggage, and runs errands.

butler A chief male household servant.

chambermaids Maids who take care of the bedrooms.

cricketer Someone who plays the game of cricket.

cursing Using bad language.

fresco A wall painting done on fresh plaster.

groundsman A person who looks after a large garden.

housekeeper A person employed to look after a house.

monk A man who is a member of a religious community.

moored Fastened to a boat.

outbreak A sudden occurrence of something unwelcome, such as war or disease.

pagan Not religious.

reception Where guests are received.

ship's log A record of important events in the management, operation, and navigation of a ship.

torture To punish or force someone to do or say something by causing great pain.

Further Information

Lunis, Natalie. *Eerie Inns (Scary Places)*. New York, NY: Bearport Publishing, 2014.

Ramsey, Grace. *Haunted Hotels (Yikes! It's Haunted)*. Vero Beach, FL: Rourke Educational Media, 2016.

Website

Scary for kids site with information on many haunted hotels: **www.scaryforkids.com/haunted-hotels/**

Publisher's note to educators and parents: Our editors have carefully reviewed these websites to ensure that they are suitable for students. Many websites change frequently, however, and we cannot guarantee that a site's future contents will continue to meet our high standards of quality and educational value. Be advised that students should be closely supervised whenever they access the Internet.

Index

Don't be scared! Most people don't believe ghosts are real at all. No one has ever scientifically proven they exist. But it can be fun to get yourself a little spooked!